WALLS OF CONFINEMENT

It is more than just "Church"

Rev. Mildred McMurtry

3G Publishing, Inc.
3600 Park Lake Lane
Norcross, Georgia 30092
www.3gpublishinginc.com
Phone: 1-888-442-9637

First published by 3G Publishing, Inc. 7/25/11

ISBN: 978-0-9833-544-3-7

Printed in the United States of America

3G Publishing, Inc.

TABLE OF CONTENT

INTRODUCTION

So many people are sitting Sunday after Sunday in church. They are going through the same routines and the same motions. They believe that they are "good" Christians and yet, they are dying spiritually without realizing that they are. Their belief is that they are finding their joy, sitting on the deacon board, usher board, choir, and finance committee. Believing that God will see their humble working habits. Yet we discover that these same individuals are missing the true joy that comes from God.

Amazingly, where we believe God will dwell the most, the devil sneaks right in. I have seen many people give hope up when an auxiliary of the church is silenced or as they call it "sat down". I have seen the faces when a vote or something trivial does not go their way. The good church folks, of all places, can make an individual feel hurt and broken. For these hurt individuals, not realizing that there is more to ministry than that can lead them to go into a hiatus or long term removal from their church family. These souls believe that their departure from a certain church will make their troubles go away once they have jumped ships. However, they are destined to discover that many of their problems have indeed found a way into their midst again. Many times, these individuals are still facing set issues because they do not have what they need to get through those tough times because they have relied on their church family and the pastor for way too long. Instead, they have not discovered how to make God move for them. How do I know this... because I was one of those souls!

No man can ever steal my joy or make me feel that I'm not worthy of being called a child of the most high! Thanks to God I have found a true relationship with him! Yes! I finally let go of religion and found a friend in Jesus. Indeed, he met me just where I was. I have a relationship with him now and I love every moment I spend with him!

My prayer is that as you read this book, my story, you will find comfort in knowing that whether you attend a church on a regular basis, chose not to go to church at all, or just attend on special occasions; the most important thing is that you get to know Jesus on a personal level as your friend in deed. If you are bound by tradition, rules and bi-laws from religion and legalism, know that:

The Son therefore shall make you free, ye shall be free indeed. John 8:36KJVk

CHAPTER 1
YOU MUST GO TO CHURCH

Wake up y'all, let's go, it is time for church! Hurry up, get your clothes on, brush your teeth, wash your face, and get the comb, I need to hurry and comb your hair. We are leaving in thirty minutes....

I heard these words every Sunday morning—It was a glorious chaotic time. There was no discussion you were going to church. This was the day that everyone in the house (parents mind you) was the happiest and most kind-hearted people in the world. It seemed as if our house was indeed the most pleasant on Sunday morning, more so than any of the other days of the week. My entire family would pile into the car and head for church. What surprised me the most was that some days during the week, we hardly had enough food to eat or gas in the car to go anywhere. Yet on Sunday, there was always plenty of gas. In addition, unbelievably, we could, most of the times, get a sausage biscuit from Ms. Winners for breakfast. What was going on? Was Sunday some kind of magical day; was this the only day that you could get a blessing from the Lord?

I looked at all my friends living around me in the housing projects. They were at home, sleeping, watching television not making any plans to attend church. Looking out the window at my neighbors in my hood, they seem to have no care for putting on the "frilly" dresses, suits, ties or shining shoes; however, they appeared to be more blessed than we were. But how? I questioned. They are not giving God any time of day.

Looking back on it, I arrived at the conclusion, that there was no excuse that these individuals were not going to church. Especially, when I gathered, that there was a church right in the neighborhood, right on the corner of the street. So I fathomed that they should have somewhere to go.

In my child's mind, I was confused. My family would drive twenty-three miles to our church home in Hiram. Not a pleasant drive always. My brothers and I would always fight, or get carsick every now and then... but for what?

Were we better than those folk at home because we were going to church in a nearby city? Were we better because we were going at all?

Now, I must say that I loved seeing my cousins and friends at church. This was our time to laugh and "pick" at people. Anyone can tell you that I would always find something to laugh about. See that was what church was to me. In Sunday school, we were taught and we learned as best as we could, from whoever would put up with us. Most of the time it was someone we figured didn't know as much as we did.

Many times, we would sit and hear the adults arguing in their classes. As I remember, I could not understand why there were two adult classes, class #7 and class #8. The people in those classes were like night and day. My father was in class #8 and they were the ones who would raise their voices the most and have the most disagreements. Now, my mother's was in class #7, they were very mild mannered. They seem to believe and accept whatever was told to them.

I loved the choir. I loved singing more than I can tell you. This was me! This was where I felt close to God. This was the area in which my siblings and I took more seriously inside of the entity of the church. But for me, I still felt that something was still missing. It was church we were there and that was that, or so it appeared.

On Sunday morning, it was always the same routines: devotion, song, scripture, announcements, offering, alter call, song and then the sermon. The repetitiveness and redundancy was leading to boredomness.com; of which of course, my friends and I pounced on the opportunity the second we stepped into the sanctuary. I can remember standing in the foyer of the church waiting to go inside the choir stand. We would laugh because someone, anyone, would mimic the deacons praying. We knew every word that would come out of their mouths, because it was the same prayer Sunday after Sunday. Word for word. Now was this a rehearsed prayer like those rehearsed choir songs, or did God place the same words in their hearts to pray every Sunday? Did it even matter to them?

Sermon time meant sleep time, especially for the dull unending praying deacons. It was talk time for us, overly eager "church to be done" children, in the choir. Amongst our talking, babies cried, there was gum popping, and the finance committee in the back room counting money and arguing over the amount. It was a wonder the preacher could think, let alone preach. The finance committee, hid behind their positions, staying in the back room forever not caring what the preacher was preaching. But that was still O.K. just as long as we were there in that so-called sanctified place called church.

For us children sometimes, Church meant a collateral truce—our bodies here for our freedom later. The rule in the house was if you didn't go to church you couldn't go skating that Sunday night. Our constant chatter was us letting each other know what we were going to wear to the skating rink that night and what time we would be there. Amazingly, while were setting up our date nights, we also could see the dread on other kids faces that were preparing for the "Doors of the Church to be opened". If it was a child, you could bet it's because the parent made them come. Yes indeed, I did say made them!

I remember waking up one Sunday morning and my mother coming into my room telling me "Missy, today you are going to join the church". I was terrified. No discussion, just you are going to do it or you knew what you would get. Was this the way to accept Christ?

I cried all the way to church. There was no joy or laughter in me that Sunday and as far as I was concerned. I could have cared less about getting to go skating either. All I could think about was stepping out in front of those people to say yes to whatever the preacher asked whether I understood what he was saying or not.

When the time came, I stepped to the front, sat in the chair scared to death crying my eyes out. I remember the pastor saying "Look at those tears she's crying tears of joy". WHAT? I heard my brain say behind tear-filled eyes. Those were tears of fear and intimidation, not of joy and happiness. They were tears of torture and begging the question to when can I get out of here!

I said yes to the questions the preacher asked and than he did something that I will never forget, something that didn't feel appropriate with me then and to this day, I still have a problem with. After all that agony I went through, he stopped to ask the deacons, "what do I hear deacons, do we accept her as a candidate for baptism? Now, I am thinking, you mean to tell me my mother made me come, I'm scared and now it's up to "these" deacons, the ones my father would call drinkers, gamblers, and just no good men?. They were the ones who would determine whether or not I was baptized. Lord please let them say NO! I thought to myself in a sarcastic manner.

What is wrong with this picture? Maybe nothing, we were at church and that was all that mattered.

CHAPTER 2

AFTER CHURCH

In the car on the way to grandma's house, all I could think about was thanking God this is over. I've now "joined the church" as my mama wanted. My parents are very happy and At least I got something good out of the deal, I'm definitely going skating. Not only that, at least my death sentence allows me a good meal at grandma's. I wondered the rest of the way about what good food grandma has cooked. I salivate at the idea of her making a pound cake.

The Church antics would continue at grandma's house. My parents and the rest of the adults later would all talk about the conference that was announced for next Saturday and laugh at sister "So-n-so" who shouted today and fell on brother "So-n-so". I began to realize the comedic affects of churchgoers. Not one mentioned what the sermon was about, let along a glorious "OH YEAH! The choir sang great today".

My grandmother's church wasn't any better. It would not get any better. She would discuss the things that were happening there. Nothing good would ever be mentioned, just the bad. All I wanted to do was just eat so this experience would be over and we could just leave. My father would only stay a minute and then off he would go to drink and gamble with cousins and friends. All of this after "church".

Now do not get me wrong, I share this so that you can see the impact this had on me and I'm sure plenty of others. I do not believe that people are bad or evil on the account of the after church special. However, I feel that there should never be an after church special—there is no need. If you received your gifts directly. Thank God that this did not settle in my spirit. The fulfillment of God's experiences should over ride much of these happenings that I have experienced. If this sounds familiar to you and this is something you are doing, I pray that at this very moment you are being convinced that this is not the way. As I got older and could understand the underground world of "Church folks" there were always times in my life that I knew there had to be more than what I was experiencing. I desired to feel the power of God's spirit.

During the week when there was no Church service there was an elderly lady named Ms. Florene, that lived in my neighborhood who would bring her grandchildren, me, and other's into her home and teach us God's word and pray with us. She even taught us to pray individually. This meant the world to me because she allowed us to pray in our own way. She didn't make us feel as if we were too young to talk to God or that what we had to say didn't matter. These were prayers that were from our hearts, not prayers we heard someone else pray! I begin to wonder how Ms. Florene could know so much about the Lord when I never saw her go to church. Actually, she couldn't because she was taking care of her mentally disabled granddaughter. How could God be in this house? I thought he only attended the church house, my church. Surely, he couldn't be here in this house with this old woman and these little "bad" children. But believe it or not, I could truly feel his presence during our bible study lesson and prayer time. I could feel it there, yet I couldn't feel his presence at church.

These events happened in my life on more than one occasion. Some of my most precious encounters with the Lord were either on the street passing by, talking with someone or in the presence of people at a restaurant or in someone's home. Most times it was with people who couldn't or wouldn't go to church for whatever reason.

CHAPTER 3
CHURCH BLINDNESS

Now do not misunderstand me, I enjoyed going to church most of the time, but as I said, it was only because of the choir.

As a young adult, and shortly after I was called into the ministry, God moved me into other areas of ministry that did not include singing in the choir. I was hurt and even upset for a while not fully understanding where he would lead me. Eventually, he manifested himself for me and I understood why. As I look back on his movement, those times where the times of picking and competition. I was being guided to see the true revelation of his form, and to fully understand how out of sync our ideas are with what we believe he wants us to do. For example, when we would go off to sing at Choir Explosions the performances and competition seemed to be about more than giving glory to God. It was more so whose choir was "raising the roof", if you know what I mean. The best way to know that your choir sung the best, was by how many people would stand up and clap or if someone would "shout". I remember how we would feel if no one stood up for us. We would be devastated!

We would argue with one another saying things like, "you were singing out of tune" or "we shouldn't have sung that song, that other choir sung it better than we did". Lo and behold, if you were the one leading the song and we fell flat, everybody would be upset with you and would talk about you. Now, the flip side of that would be if your choir blew it out of the water, you would get the highest praises from everyone near and far; which made you feel like a superstar. Chest stuck out, everybody congratulating you, (you taking all God's glory) and your choir definitely on the receiving end of another invite to perform for sure.

In retrospect, how bad it was to realize if it weren't for the Lord, we would not have sounded good and would not have done so well. We took his glory and never recognized him at all. Believe me when I say, those shouts came from the beat of the music not the moving of the spirit. Did we just not know any better? Did we not even care? Everyone was doing it and that's the way it was.

CHAPTER 4
DO NOT BE A FOLLOWER

Do not get complacent with that's the way it was or is. If it's not God's way than it's not the way it is. It's not good to be a follower!

When I met my husband, his family was not sure if I was the one for him. They felt because I lived in the "projects" that I was one of those "fast" girls. One Sunday at a nearby Church, our church choir attended a musical. I was shocked to see my now mother and sister-in-law sitting there with their children's choir. I was scared to death because I was going to lead one of the songs. I belted out "Bread of Heaven" as if my life depended on it. When my in-laws heard me sing, you would have thought I gave them a million dollars. I received the grandest hugs from both of them and everyone in the church stood up that Sunday for us. I was so proud that day. I remember everyone saying, "Missy, girl you got down today", "You tore that church up". My husband, then boyfriend, called me that night and told me how much his mother talked about me singing in the choir. I remember him saying, "If they didn't like you before they love you now. You are in the church and that makes them real happy". *WOW!* I thought blankly to myself. *I'm in the church, so what! I could have been the biggest rebellious, pot smoking; liquor drinking two-faced liar and they would not have cared as long as I was going to church. That's all that mattered!* I continued our conversation and pretended that everything was all right. Realizing all the while that wrong was exactly the answer to my actions.

What exactly is wrong here? I'll tell you what's wrong, with this picture. There was poor judgment, no spiritual discernment or insight, lack of wisdom and knowledge, just a body going to a church building. And the funny thing is, when I was going to church just playing along, I was loved beyond measures. However, when I matured spiritually in my walk with God and began a relationship with him, I am disliked more now than ever.

When I got married, I joined my husband's church so that our entire family could fellowship in one place. Big mistake! I begin to go, my husband stopped going, and things were worst in this place of worship than in my home church. I have never seen so much hypocritical, traditional bondage and legalistic bunch of churchgoers in my life. You were talked about if you didn't wear white on communion Sunday. If you didn't contribute the right dollar amounts to the various church functions such as anniversary gatherings or friends and family day your name was condemned basically to the bowels of hell—you were not worthy if you were not a cheerful giver. Whatever the value committed, you'd better pay what you were suppose to pay or your name was called out in front of the whole congregation and guest, therefore you were embarrassed. If you missed any church services or functions, you'd better be sick in bed or on your deathbed. Twenty years and eight preachers later it's still the same way. It reminds me of the scripture:

Isaiah chapter 1: 13 when God said he could not endure anymore!

The depravity of it all, all of those conferences and meetings proved to be of ill affect. There was one meeting I remember very well. Some of the members were angry because they felt the preacher liked one group of members more than the other. All of this was because this group of members named their choir after the preacher. I had never seen so much jealousy and confusion in my life. I wondered what in the world was God saying when he looked down on such mess and disarray. Fighting over the preacher's name! Isn't the only name that truly matters the name of Jesus?

At one meeting the members decided to vote the preacher out. They didn't want him anymore. And let me tell you, the church was packed. It was more people at this meeting than during church services. Reality TV in reality, so to speak. One of the members got up and told the preacher to leave the church. She bluntly told him that they didn't want him anymore. "I'm not going anywhere" he responded with conviction. She then responded, "You are out of here". This death match went back and forth for a good hour. Nothing was resolved that night. The decision was split down the middle. But that next day at service, the preacher got up, preached like never before and then told the congregation if they didn't want him he would leave.

I admired him for that, and to this day I still have so much respect for him. I was given the opportunity to come to his new church and preach on several occasions. This was at least eighteen years later. There he was in a new church with the same choir and doing great!

I laugh now when I think about being in the midst of that nonsense, and what's sad about it is that there are churches now going through the same form of issues. I learned a valuable lesson then that it doesn't pay to fight with church folk. Dust your feet off and keep stepping as the word says: *And whoever will not receive you nor hear your words, when you depart from that house or city, shake off the dust from your feet" Matt 10: 13. Believe me; God will take care of your enemies.*

Wake up my brother and sister's! If you find yourself planning any types of "lynch mob meetings" you better think about changing it to a praise meeting! I have been in more meetings to get rid of preachers than I care to count. I felt nasty, dirty and disgusted then and I still do not feel 100% clean even though I know that God has forgiven me. If you are in this type of situation now, run for your life. You are on dangerous grounds and when that ground collapse you are going to collapse right along with it the word of God clearly says, *Do not touch My anointed ones, And do My prophets no harm. 1Ch 16:22*

What's going on? What's happening in these four walls? Are you sitting Sunday after Sunday taking up space waiting for the next church meeting? When I think about the inside of those church walls, I think about giving God praise and glory. It's all about him and not about us. He set's the order, we follow his leading and not do what we want and expect him to clean up our mess. I do not remember anything other than God's business in the temple except one time and that's when Jesus came in angry and turned over tables because they were selling.

In Matt 21:12 *Then Jesus went into the temple of God and drove out all those who bought and sold in the temple, and overturned the tables of the money changers and the seats of those who sold doves.* Now, how many fish fry, barbeque and pork chitterling plates have you brought from the church?

Seeking and searching was where I found myself. I could not find peace where I was so I set out to find that closeness' with the Father. I wanted him to call me daughter. I wanted to make sure he knew my name when I called on him. Can you imagine God having this conversation with Jesus, "Who's that trying to pray"; I do not know that person". Jesus would reply..."I think they sing in the choir on Sunday, meet with the ushers on 1st Saturday and hold a position as the clerk of the church, I've heard them critique the pastor's sermon on several occasions but I can't remember them spending any time in the word or with us. Maybe they're too BUSY!

Doesn't this make you wonder and take a good long look into the mirror to see if everything's alright with you? Right?

CHAPTER 5

STARTING GROUND

I have a good friend who attended a very small church in which they held their church services; in fact this place of worship was a trailer. I visited with her during several Sunday morning services. The people were so fired up, or should I say on fire for God that I thought I was in literally in heaven.

The gifts of the spirit were being manifested in a powerful way. I was impressed. No signs of shame. People were professing Jesus as their Savior, confessing their sins and being delivered, speaking in tongues, interpretation of tongues, teaching the word, praising God, worshipping, I couldn't believe it. These few people were having some serious church services.

I started attending regularly, Sunday after Sunday. I was getting very comfortable being with the members. I did not want to get too involved, I just wanted to sit and soak in all of what the Lord had planned for me. But you know how that goes…. You can only attend a church for a while and then the pressure turns on you to join. About two months after, the overseer called me out one Sunday. She told the congregation that she was impressed with my singing but singing would not get me into heaven, I needed to be saved. What she said didn't bother me because; I had always felt that I had not truly accepted Jesus as my Savior. I was comfortable and trusted that the spirit was revealing the truth about me. Remembering the episode at my home church when I was younger and how I joined there, it just didn't seem complete.

After confessing Jesus as my Savior and repenting of my sins, I was baptized all over again. Growing up in the South, studies have shown that the most segregated day of the week, happens to be on Sundays. So to my shock, the baptism took place at a non-black church at that juncture, I had never seen whites and blacks worship together. I remember coming up out of the water speaking in an unknown tongue. My mouth was moving fifty miles an hour. I felt so renewed. I felt like I became a new person.

Shortly after that, my son who was around ten years old came to me and

said he wanted to be saved. He didn't want to go to hell. He had seen the movie "Left Behind" and it really made an impact on his life. I was determined that my children would not have the same experience as I did and I prayed that they would come to me, and that I not force them to accept Jesus. I couldn't believe the changes that were taking place in my life. Some were good changes and some were not so good. I started speaking boldly against things I didn't believe in which was a good thing to me but, judging by my friends and family's responses, there were some not so good things I was doing, like hurting family members, neglecting my husband and home. I was doing this because I did not have the spiritual maturity. I was over zealous with little wisdom and a critical spirit. I just plunged into this newfound "religion" that I had no balance and neither did they. My whole world started to evolve around this church and the people. Unfortunately, this went on for two years and then it happened, the people started to act like those of old days. Evidently, I had gotten so close to God and/or "slipped" up and prayed for wisdom that I believe he heard me because the overseer started preaching Sunday after Sunday about makeup, pants and jewelry. I thought "what in the world does this have to do with my salvation or my relationship with God. I didn't wear too much makeup, I only wore small gold hoop earrings, which was all I could afford and I didn't wear tight pants because I was too large to get into spandex so what was the big deal? I started searching the bible like crazy to see what scriptures supported this teaching because the scriptures they were giving didn't coincide with what they were saying. I wasn't about to take off my earrings and makeup, my hair was short and I probably would look like a man if I didn't accessorize. However, I ended up following suit. Furthermore, in the back of my mind I knew my husband liked the way I looked, he wanted me to look nice, and surely God didn't have a problem with me pleasing my husband.

This church appeared to be the best thing to ever happen to us. I begin to think about all the wonderful things I experienced and heard about at this church: The leader had been healed from cancer, my good friend's baby, who weighed only one pound and some ounces at birth, was manifested into a strong healthy child after many prayers and anointing. My own son was even healed from asthma after the overseer laid hands on him. I received the understanding and gladness that I know now that God can use whom he pleases but the power comes from him. I also remember loosing time at work and the church blessed me financially with the exact amount missing from my check. How in the world could they have known that! I couldn't believe it and neither could my husband. All these positive events and now the legalism! My heart was broken! It didn't stop; the more I went to church the more the sermons were condemning. We were condemned for everything, which was everyone there except the family members. I even begin to see some things that I never paid any attention to before. There were no men at this church. Only about two men and the rest were women. Where were the husbands? We all had them and mine wouldn't come either.

My family called the church a cult. I never thought of it that way, but after thinking long and hard and praying about the situation, I didn't care if it was a cult or not it was time for me to "jet" and I did. They were very upset when I left. They even tried for a while to find out where I had gone. When they finally found me, I was back at my home church, singing and directing the choir, wearing makeup and jewelry, thinking things would be better, instead I was going backwards instead of forward.

About twelve years after leaving the church, the overseer passed away. My friend, who also left a year after me, and I went to the funeral home to pay our last respects. When we went into the room to view her remains, I became ill. I begin to feel so sick and weak as if there was an evil presence in the room. I decided not to go any farther, my friend also left out. On the way home we never spoke a word about how we felt until a few days later. We were talking and I couldn't resist asking her what happened. She told me she felt exactly the same way. She said it bothered her so that she talked to her husband about it. Her son, the one the who was born a preemie and also who to this day is an awesome man of God told her that the overseer died with resentment in her heart over his mother leaving the church. The first thing I thought was how in the world would this child know this, but at the same time I knew he was telling the truth, it was full confirmation of what I believed, except when I told my husband I said to him "Mothers (overseer) gone but she left here still angry with me".

At this juncture, I am thinking, I'm so glad to be back at my home church, excited about being this new creature in Christ. I felt I knew who I was, saved and filled with the Holy Spirit, washed in the blood of the Lamb. I plunged back into church work not long after returning. I wanted to make a difference in the lives of others this time. Be a part of a solution instead of part of any problems. I knew the church was not use to seeing the gifts of the spirit manifest, it would take some time for them to vigilant but I was prayerful and hopeful. One Sunday one of the members came up to me, and asks where I had been. After telling her, she said to me "Well, wherever you have been I want to go and get some of what you got". I told her to just trust in God and believe and that change would come. I felt very good at the fact that she and others could see the change in my life. I definitely didn't want to go into details what had happen I just wanted to remember the awesome things God had done for me while I was there.

I stayed at church, especially, at choir rehearsal. I was back to enjoying every minute of it. I even found myself working with every choir in the church, even the male chorus. We had a good musician and each choir was pretty full. I was feeling great. Things were better much better at home and I was just having a great time. I was still a member of my husband's church, we were visiting there every once in a while but I was happy were I was.

The funny thing is when I did finally rejoin my home church, a letter was sent (I found out later) telling not asking, the pastor to send me back to my former church because I had unfinished business there. What a laugh! How in the world are you going to make somebody come back to your church when they do not want to? My mother told me that the pastor had a letter sent back to them saying he would not suggest for me to return, it was my decision only.

The response led me to a conversation I had with a friend that has a prophetic gift. My friend said the church he left came and told him he had not sent them a letter saying he was not returning to church. His response to them was of course a sarcastic tone stating "didn't the spirit tell you I wasn't coming back; since ya'll so spiritual you should have heard in the spirit"! Can you believe it, church folk!

So everything seemed to be fine. The church even offered me $75.00 a month to be the director all the choirs of the church. But looking back, I wished I never agreed to that. That became the beginning of more problems than ever. I thought the extra money was a blessing, but more hell came with that money than blessings. All of a sudden another member wanted to work with one of the choirs. Well, I had no problem sharing the job, but after doing the job for a month, she and her family members wanted to know how come she wasn't getting paid as well. No doubt, she could have use the money just as much as me but some of the members didn't feel she was "qualified" to receive that money. Most of them didn't even think she had any business directing the choir when she was living with her children's father and not married.

My point is this: Why squabble over something so trivial. Especially, in the house of the Lord. We were bashing this woman who had faults but whose faults were no different than yours or minds. The issues from these squabbles were not merely about a woman living unwed to a man, it was more so about jealousy and envy. What about all the "sin" we do that people do not see? Do we just sweep that under the rug and pretend we're holier than thou! I was once unmarried living with my husband with a child. Just because now I'm married, does it make me any different from her? Sin is Sin!!

Unfortunately, as the well runs deep, it also runs dry as fast. When it came down to it, both of us were financially demoted. It took six months to end the whole ordeal. I'll never forget, one Sunday I went to the financial secretary and told her I had not been paid in three months. At this particular time I was really going through some financial problems and needed the money. She went in and spoke with the finance committee and shortly came out and handed me a check for that month and the past two months. It wasn't five minutes later that another finance member came out to my car and made the statement to me that the church had to write out more checks that day than they brought in money. Now either she thought I was stupid and would not figure out that she was talking about me, or she really was trying to say to me I should give the money back and be a shamed for asking for it.

After that I didn't receive another check from the church and I never asked for it again. From that time and even now, it is so hard for me to accept any type of payment, love offering for church work from any church. I realized that although the monetary gifts can be a blessing, but with it comes responsibility and a full heart. From then on, I was thankful to provide my own gifts of love but understanding that my blessings would fall in my lap in some other form and fashion.

I kept serving as choir director and attending services regularly. I didn't let this incident bother me. My spiritual relationship with the leaders of the church were becoming stronger. The pastor would consult me on different matters concerning programs, etc. Everything was fine, I thought and then one Sunday I came to church, everyone was quiet, noticeably quiet, not speaking to one another. I later found out that at the conference the night before, which I had decided a long time ago, that I would never attend, the pastor got upset with one of the members. He called her a "trouble maker" and said some other things to her. You can imagine my surprise when I found out it was the same member that (in so many words) said I broke the church. I thought to myself: she is a troublemaker, and she was told what she deserves. But of course, the "lynch mob" was forming and the pastor was on his way out the door!

Wait a minute- hold the press! The pastor has to go because he called someone a "trouble maker". What about Jesus when he told the disciples "how long am I to trouble with you". (Matthew 17:17). Did they want to dismiss Jesus, get rid of him for telling the truth?

After many, long meetings or disagreements you could say, the pastor decided to leave. Fifteen years of service and this one incident gets him kicked out. I was furious. What about forgiving and forgetting? Was he not human also? Was he not allowed of being angry? Or even was he not allowed to make any mistakes, can we move on and forget the past? Not so, the pastor was out and we found ourselves looking for another one.

The church received many resumes' from preachers all over. They each came in and did their performances Sunday after Sunday. I was on the committee to help choose the "right man" for the job. I didn't want that job and if it had not been for my mother pushing me I would not have accepted it. (How many times have you done something to please someone else when you knew it was wrong?)

The committee must have realized I didn't care because they barely called me for meetings and never asked my opinion. When we would talk individually with the potential pastors the right questions were never asked and half the time we never knew what in the world they were saying. All the committee wanted to know is if they could fill the church, more people meant more money. When I finally opened my mouth to speak, I asked the church could we come together and have a shut in prayer session so that we all could hear from God in this situation and in hopes that we could all get on one accord. There were over fifty people in the meeting when I asked, they all agreed but when the time came to pray only four attended. Myself, the associate pastor, who also wanted the church, one other member who felt the same as I did and wouldn't you know it the so-called "trouble maker". We prayed until one o'clock in the morning. I really prayed to God on behalf of the church and all I could hear was "I'll send you a leader".

The sad thing is we had a pastor there. He was young and maybe a little inexperience, but he was open to learning all he needed to know. But of course the church continued to accept resumes', listening to different preachers, having meetings until finally they had two candidates and the church was ready to vote. I went to the meeting to vote for the pastor but I refuse to vote. I was asked to count the ballets along with two deacons. With the new pastor barely getting the majority vote they got what they thought they needed and I do say "they" because I didn't vote and I surely didn't agree.

Father, please tell me what and why the church was established? Is it to do your will or our own? Are you really please with the way we are handling things in the church? More, more of you Lord. I want more of you, more of your power, more of your anointing, more of your strength, just more of you Lord.

CHAPTER 6

FINDING CHURCH

A lot came to light at the first bible meeting with the new pastor. One of the deacons, one that had been a deacon for several years, ask the questions "Who is God really, where did he come from". My heart dropped! My thoughts, *here are men that were carrying on in the absence of the pastor that do not even know who God really is.* The Father we prayed to Sunday after Sunday. I do give him credit for asking the questions. Some would be embarrassed and would keep on living with that lack of knowledge.

The pastor gave an answer and told the congregation that we would begin the bible study by starting at the very beginning. Good move! This is what many of us have wanted to do for so long. He begins "In the Beginning". What a great place to start, maybe this pastor knows what he is doing, he sees the need, is trying to meet them and then it happened. About a month after the pastor was there, he and I had a conversation about the church and ways to improve some of the areas. I was honored that my opinion mattered to him. Then he made a statement that he was working with and I quote "a bunch people that didn't know nothing, what was ya'll doing before I came because nothing is in order". Now, I will admit, there were places that needed work, but the church was not in that bad of shape, and I couldn't help but wonder was I apart of these people that didn't know anything.

That hurt me so much. I was even somewhat afraid of being manipulated, so I started going after God diligently. I didn't want to miss anything and I wasn't going to let myself be destroyed for lack of knowledge. As sad as it was, not knowing any better the church members were setting themselves up to be used and abused.

Well enough of that, this is about me right! I'm not here to judge! So with the new pastor, things seemed to move forward. Classes were being offered on a regular basis, they even offered a Saturday class. Which I attended believe it or not. I was diving into the word, wanting more and more. After sometime I thought this is all right and then back to the same ole, same ole.

It started to seem that without mess the church could not function. When I say mess that's what it was. Let me give you an example, the pastor called a meeting with the senior choir after church one Sunday because of some friction. Now do not get me wrong, I know there's always going to be problems especially when there are a lot of people involved, but when this "pastor" addressed the matter he made the statement that "we use to be the top choir when he first came, but now we were going down"! What in the world is a top choir? This came from an educated doctrinal pastor. I could not believe my ears. Why he was even involved with such petty mess in the first place? This goes back to saying things were a mess there. At least the pastor before had deacons assigned to each auxiliary in the church that would handle situation as this, but this man is getting involved with mess and you know what happened the next Sunday, he preached about it! There was no one interested in the choir friction any more they were now upset about that crazy comment. He just added to the problem!

That was just the beginning. There were other problems such as, the mother board got upset with some of the members, namely children, who didn't pay to eat breakfast at one of their function before service one Sunday, in the church mind you, where they were raising money for **themselves**. This should have made me more upset than them, especially when I found out that one of those children was my own, and I should have turned those tables over just like Jesus did for them selling in the church. One of the mothers even turned one child away and did not allow them to eat until the mother brought them the money. Not me of course, when I saw what was happening I told my children to get out of line and we went to Martin's restaurant and got a biscuit.

This is when I stop criticizing "bench warming members", because that's what I was about to become a sit down, go home, not participate, only see me on Sunday, loose my telephone number, eat at home, uninvolved Christian!

I'm glad I've learned the only service God requires of me is to believe in his Son Jesus, love him, and love my neighbors feed the hungry, give to the poor and pray for the sick. That I can do although hard at times but I can do it!!!

CHAPTER 7

BREAKING FREE

But of course, I was not about to become that person. I felt too much guilt just to sit down on the church. I believe I was confined to the four walls, going through all this unnecessary garbage Sunday after Sunday.

My heart began to say what my mind was telling me. There are people all around me needing help. What's wrong with me? Am I really confined to staying in these four walls? Would God be unpleased with me if I chose to go outside these walls and help other people?

There were people all around me that could dissect the word of God with ease. I could plainly see that there were good people who not only talked the talk but walked the walk. They were Christians who had dedicated their lives to living that Christ-like life. Prayer Warriors who were willing to stick with you through any situation. They did not have ulterior motives or wanted to waste time on trivial problems or foolish antics. Yes God, this is what I want to do I proclaimed to him. This is the need I have to help others, not just singing in the choir, coming up with ways to raise money to build a new building, or buy new choir robes. I need TO BE REAL for you God.

The more time I dedicated myself to studying and prayer, and especially to praise and worship, I could hear so clearly from the Lord. It wasn't easy though, the enemy attacked me on every side but it didn't matter because I was developing a relationship with God and I knew he would fight every battle for me. I was talked about and ridiculed but that didn't stop me. No more of this religion and tradition of feeling bad if I didn't have white to wear on communion Sunday, or if I gave all that I had at anniversaries instead of the "set" amount. I was FREE!

During this time I had an opportunity to attend a women's conference that was so powerful I couldn't believe it. The anointing was so heavy you felt as if you were literally drunk. I could hardly stand up straight. I went to the class "Hearing the Voice of God" where I met a woman by the name of Mother Rose. By this time I was a licensed minister. She even said to me "you're a minister aren't you", and she had never met me before. As a matter of fact, I didn't know any of the women there except for the one that gave me the invitation to come and I only met her one time at a church I was visiting the week before. I was thinking, I refuse to go to another conference or church meeting! I tried to get someone to go with me. I would have paid her way but no one was available. I decided not go, got back in bed and the spirit spoke as clear as a bell, Go! So I got up and went.

In the class, Mother Rose said to me that the devil was trying to kill me with heart problems. She said that the Lord had work for me to do and the devil wanted to kill me. She proceeded to say, "I hear the Lord saying too fast for three days, on these days also take communion. Well, my first thought was, no way, I'm not an ordained minister. Only ordained ministers are allowed to touch communion. I'm not getting in trouble with the Lord!

Now what Mother Rose didn't know was, I had had a physical earlier that week and sure enough the doctor called that Monday after the conference and said that I needed to go for more test. Indeed, something was going on with my heart. You better know I didn't think twice about fasting those three days and taking that communion. By the grace of God, I took an echogram that week and the next week the nurse called and said that the test came out perfect. I raised the roof in praise to God for what he had done. The next day a different nurse called with the same results. I told her that someone had already called and told me, she apologize and hung up. The very next day a different nurse called and told me the same thing, when I told her I had already been called twice she said "well I guess the news is so good you have to hear it three times. I said "Yea, one for the Father one for the Son and one for the Holy Spirit and I praise God even the more!!!

I shared this experience with some of my friends and family later on and unfortunately they looked at me crazy. Some even made negative comments, but you know what, obedience is better than sacrifice (1 Samuel 15:22), and I would rather be obedient to the Lord and sacrifice my reputation, family and friends relationship than to be disobedient guessing everything and missing my blessings.

Clearly, I was blessed! Truly Blessed! Even now when I feel a little pain here or there, or feel irregular heartbeats, or when I go to the doctor and he orders EKG's, I remember I am HEALED!! No weapon formed against me shall prosper (Isaiah 54:17)! I got scared really bad one time and I started to pray and I heard the Lord say, "I only have to heal you once my child, get up!"

That blew me away. I had to stop worrying about that situation and trust God. That came true for a lot of situations. There were times I was holding on to things and people that the Lord was saying let go of. Doing things that were unfulfilling, I had no joy in doing them but I kept right doing it out of obligations. I was dealing with folks that were hindering my growth: yet in still, I was going after God with all my might. The funny thing was, I didn't have to follow a certain program, or formula that had been set up all I had to do was surrender myself to God's will. So I would submit and commit to his ways, spend quality time in worship and prayer. A lot of times I just sat quietly and listened to what the spirit had to say to me.

So when I would hear the Lord say let a certain things go or separate myself from someone or somebody's, I didn't hesitate. There were those times when I wanted to remove myself from situations and I would be led to stay in it. But that was O.K.! God always gave me double for my trouble and learning my lesson was my salvation`.

CHAPTER 8

HAVING CHURCH OR NOT

Home church became our Sunday morning routine. I would listen well to the spirit of the Lord and however he led me that's what I did. It was wonderful sitting at the table with my family, singing praying and studying the word. It was awesome! I remember the Lord leading me to have my oldest son teach on Sunday. He taught out of the book of Matthew. His subject was "God shall supply all our needs" He started off by asking do we believe the word of God. We all answered, "Yes". His next statement was then why do we worry? It only took him ten minutes to teach/ preach and he didn't sway one time from the bible. He got straight to the point and didn't miss a beat. We all left the table so blessed, so refreshed with a word that still has an impact on our lives. I remember saying to my husband later that day "it do not take God long to do nothing" "it doesn't take God long to do anything? You see I didn't' have to sing a song to death or sing six or seven songs or pray for an hour for God to show up. We all came to receive and that's what we did receive!

Speaking of singing to death, when I think of all the time I spent in choirs singing, singing, singing, I could have spent of lot of that time studying to show myself approved (2 Timothy 2:15). Now, I know some of you can relate to this. Only the best singers could sing before the pastor preaches. If a song didn't sound too good we would sing that one during offering when no one was paying much attention. And if the leader messed up, everyone would be so upset with them, almost to the point of being talked about so bad until feelings were hurt.

It was such a part of me, as a matter a fact at one point I was so involved in it that I started attending classes each year that taught on choir etiquette. I would bring what I learned back to the choir and make some suggestions, such as no wearing pants in the choir, no jewelry when wearing the choir robes and if you were late on Sunday morning you couldn't come in the choir stand at all. Things I thought would really help the choir and get us structured. One Saturday at rehearsal I remember mentioning to the young adult choir the "no pants" rule. You would have thought I told those girls to come naked!

I may sound as if I'm putting down church and the choir, I do know each has a purpose in this life time and I do realize we have to have a place to worship and I know the word says forsake not the assembly of believers to come together and praise God (Hebrews 10:25). But, I also know that church has been a place of hurt and hard times for many. The point I want to get across is that many have walked away from the church hurt and went back out into the world thinking that without the church they have no hope, sinners lost. Not true. Let's set the record straight here and now. Just because you find yourself not in a church home or to say it plain have your name on somebody's church roll, does not mean you cannot be or are not saved. My family and I went to church EVERY SUNDAY and knew we were not saved any more than the man on the streets. That's why it didn't surprise me when my sister told me she got saved on the way to work. No, she should have been already saved as much as we stayed in church. You see she was like me. You go through the motions but you're really not saved. When you are truly saved there's a difference in your life. You can tell there has been a change in your behavior, your attitude and it's not this thing that makes you believe you're better than everybody else, it's just the opposite. You begin to look at yourself as God shows you yourself. You become humble, your needs become second and all you want to do is help someone else. You're only concerned about doing what's right in the eyes of the Lord.

The bibles say's to be saved you must confess with your mouth, believe in your heart that God raised Jesus from the dead and you SHALL be saved (Roman 10:9). Now what part of that did it say give God your heart and the preacher your right hand and the church give you the right hand of fellowship. You do not owe the preacher or the church anything. All to (God) I owe! Give God back everything he's given you! Believe it or not you already belong to him, he just want you to give yourself freely to him. You do not have to do anything else. Jesus did it all for you when he died on the cross. Stop letting man make you feel you owe them something. What price did they pay, what blood did they shed. Jesus gave his life freely for you and me. Just trust him. If you believe he did confess your sins and live for Christ. Not the preacher, not church, not mama or daddy, sister or brother. Just live for Christ! Paul said not I but Christ that lives in me (Galatians 2:20). Do what you know is right and stop living in bondage with no freedom, confined to something that has no life and that's not going anywhere.

So what happened with my sister? She said she heard something on the radio that touched her heart like never before. It caused a life changing experience and she knew at that moment she had to be saved. She begins to confess Jesus as her Savior and repented of wrongdoing. She said the anointing fell on her so strong that she had to pull over the car. From that time and even now she takes her walk with the Lord very serious. She knows what her purpose in life is and she won't allow anyone to tell her she's not a child of the King!

When you know that you know the truth in your heart, no one can put doubt in you mind, not even Satan or his followers. Believe me, old things have passed away and behold all things become new (2 Corinthians 5:17)!

Now when I attend church I have to sometimes get in my own world when that "nonsense stuff" starts taking place.

I was invited to a women's day with a friend at her church. She was singing in the choir for the first time and she really wanted me to come and hear this choir. Against my better judgment I went. Sure enough, this choir took over the service. I told my friend I would have to leave by 9:30a, this was the 8:00am service that I was going to; she said that would be fine because they would be having Sunday school at 9:30am and she knew they would have to be out of service. That choir sung so much that when I finally left at 9:45am the guest preacher had not even preached. What was so funny on the "fast" songs the choir would sing, stop, begin again with three or more different people picking up the lead and the musician had a field day just repeating the same chorus over and over again. It got so bad until it was nerve racking! I couldn't believe it, and what was so awful was we could barely understand what they were saying. On one song (which happen to be a slow song) the leader was singing "More of you Lord" which was their theme song, she sung this song with so much feeling you could feel the anointing of God in the words and her voice. She did a great job, but the sad things was the choir barely moved or made any suggestions toward that song and only three of us stood up during the song and worshipped. The rest looked at the women as if to say "What are you singing about". Oh but when the beat started up again, everyone was up on their feet. Needless to say I didn't get a chance to hear a word from the guest preacher. When I did leave fifteen minutes late, they were introducing the church dancers. I wondered what happen to Sunday school. Later that night,

I heard from my friend. Before I could say anything she apologized for what happened.

CHAPTER 9

CHURCH DISCREPANCIES

Unfortunately these things happen in church and many other incidents. And sad to say this is why you couldn't pay many people to go to step foot in church much less to get involved.

I heard of an incident where an elderly woman was about to fight another women during church service. Her family members had to keep taking her out because she was getting so mad. Other people thought she may have been sick, well if you ask me she was sick. It was best for her to stay at home than come to church with that much anger in her. Sadly some elderly people feel that that's their church and no one is running them away from their church. They have been there for years and the church can't function without them. Do you think God is pleased with this type of behavior?

My husband has a hard time going into a church but will tell you in a minute how much he loves home church. I think he loved it more than any of us and when it came to discussing the word he knew just as much if not more than the rest of us. He was so open and seemed more relaxed at home church than I ever seen him. He was involved with church most of his life but now he refuses to get as he calls it "wrapped up in church". When I was going, I would stay on his case about attending church with me. As a matter of fact, I joined his church to be with him but he stopped going. I remember asking him why and he said "well now that you're going mama and "them" will be happy and stay off my back about going". So I was his trade!

When I first met my husband he was a junior deacon in the church. His parents were so proud of him. Little did they know he was trying his best to get out of being a deacon. He would tell me he had no business being a deacon when he was a drinker and smoker. That really bothered him. He thought he was putting a stain on the name deacon and that God was not pleased with him. Well that day came. Two years after dating I got pregnant with our first son. Even though we were not married my husband took good care of both of us and was very proud to be a daddy. I even remember him bringing lots of baby stuff to my mother's home and one of her friends, who was visiting over, heard me complaining about him bringing in so much stuff. She stopped me in my tracks and told me to "shut up" I should be glad that he was taking such good care of the baby when there were so many young girls with babies and the father's were nowhere to be found. I shut up and didn't complain again.

We took our son to church one Sunday. His daddy couldn't wait to show him off. After service the pastor asked to speak with us. When we got into his study he "lit" right into us about having children out of wedlock, unprotected sex and marriage. My husband told him we understood the circumstances and what we were facing, also that we would be good parents to our son. But according to the pastor that wasn't enough. He wanted to know when we were going to get married. After many back and forth words, the pastor told us that because we were not married our baby was a mistake. Now you have to imagine first of all we didn't expect this and secondly when he said the baby was a mistake he pointed his finger right at our son and in the same breath said that my husband could no longer be a junior deacon and not be married. So, one of our happiest moments turned into a nightmare. I burst into tears my husband stood up, grabbed the baby seat, politely cussed out the pastor and walked out. It took a long time for him to return to church even after the pastor came to his home and apologized. Makes you wonder why that saying is so true, "think before you speak".

Even after the pastor left the church, my husband's family tried so hard to get him to come back. He would visit every now and then but he never returned to any position in the church.

When the church started looking for a new pastor, my husband would read each one perfectly. He knew them inside out. It was as if after that incident he received some type of "pastor radar". He could pick out the phonies a mile away. This one pastor the church hired as an associate became good friends with me, but wouldn't you know it, my husband didn't trust him at all. He actually married us and of course my husband really didn't care for that but he was my friend so it was my decision. About three years after we were married, this pastor was arrested for child molestation. I was so hurt. My husband would often make jokes that we need to renew our vows because we were married by the devil, although I didn't see the humor in that at all, we were fooled and as far as I was concerned that was not too funny!

There's another time I almost got my husband to start coming back to church. The church called a pastor, a young man, who was well known in the community one that I had known since childhood; my husband didn't know him at all. I would speak very highly of him but my husband was skeptical because of rumors we heard of him being a homosexual. Well, I just about had him convinced that we shouldn't pay the gossip any attention when one night my husband was taking me to choir rehearsal, and Oh My God, I couldn't believe what we saw. Through the trees we could see our pastor intimately hugging another man. I tried to pretend that I didn't see it but my husband hit the roof. He was furious! He begged me not to go inside the church. He wanted me to tell the church what we had seen. Now, I'm still pretending I do not know what I saw, my husband was shouting "you know you saw those men hugging, and do not you lie and take up for that man". After we fussed a while I convinced my husband to let me go in and take care of it.

When I got into the church the pastor acted as if everything was fine. I wondered if he knew that we saw him, if he saw our headlights coming down the church path. He introduced the young man as a friend; I was still in shock but never said a word. I didn't know how to confront him with that situation and I surely wasn't going to do it in front of the church. Of course when rehearsal was over I rode to my mother-in-law's house with her. My husband was waiting on me there. The first thing he wanted to know was if I told the church. I said no, and he begins to tell his parents what we saw. He was told by his father to leave it alone they would handle it. I'm not sure what actually happened, I do know that it wasn't long after that the pastor became very ill and passed away. After his death there were six other pastors that came to the church within a three-year period. All of whom my husband did not trust, which he had good reasons not to. Another turned out to be homosexual, three others stole money from the church, another kicked my in-laws out of the church calling them trouble makers and another left because he felt he couldn't do anything with the church and it's low membership.

To this day my family names are still on the church roll there, of course we do not attend, but you know what, I'm grateful that I have come to realize it's more important to know whether or not your name is written in the Lambs Book of Life not just on a church roll.

CHAPTER 10

WHOSE CHURCH IS THE GREATEST

Now that you have read many of my "woes" one might think that I have a problem with the church. Well, I do not my problem is with the one track mind of those individuals that go to church thinking that is all that is required of them when it is not! Going to church will not save you! Please hear me well. I will probably repeat this phrase more than any other. If you are one that thinks the physical act of going to church is all that is required then, you are sadly wrong. Your seat in church does not guarantee you a seat in heaven. And if you are judging and condemning those that do not go you probably have guaranteed yourself a seat somewhere else, probably Hell! Oops! Maybe, I need to apologize. I forgot some may not believe there is a Hell. The rest, probably think that was too harsh. What I should have said is, when we judge others for not attending church we are not showing them Love and Love is exactly what will get them in the door. If you keep Love first and the nonsense at a minimal you may just keep them there. Remember, our greatest commandment was to Love!

There was a neighbor who lived right next door to me in the projects who was what we called at the time "sanctified". They never wore pants, makeup or jewelry, never cut their hair and they could not associate with certain people or go to certain functions. The family consisted of a mother, one daughter and two sons. I was very close to the daughter and my brothers were friends with the sons however, my mother and father never made friends with their mother, funny uh?

The mother didn't always trust her children to be around us because we didn't attend their church or follow their customs, if that's what you call it. I would ask the daughter all the time why and what made them so different from us and everybody else. She couldn't really answer me, I guess she didn't know or understand herself. I remember they stayed in church all the time. Their pastor was well known in the community and (of course) was well talked about. The talk was always how he would not associate with anyone else outside those in his church. However, about twenty-five years later, their church decided to build a new edifice. It was a beautiful building, very large as well. So you know large means more money, a lot more! Soon after the church was built we heard of some financial problems they were having. The pastor began to have programs to raise money to keep the church. He would invite neighboring pastors and their congregations in for different services. Of course they went but after it was said and done they couldn't wait to talk about how this pastor would ostracize them and now he needed their help. You couldn't help but believe that the talk was true. Unfortunately, they lost the church anyway and had to move back into the small church. Also sad but true the pastor died shortly thereafter. Recently I was asked to come preach at a seed faith service, they were still attempting to raise money to get back into their newer church. I never would have thought that "I" a women minister would preach in the very pulpit of a pastor who made it very clear that women should keep their place.

That reminds me of another invitation I received from a church, as a matter of fact, the church in the neighborhood I grew up in. This particular pastor really had a problem with women in the ministry. He did not have one woman on his ministerial staff. I was scared to go, so when a young woman called, I told her to call me back later that week and I would let her know. After much praying I was lead to accept the invite. For two months I thought about the service and not only that but I would rehearse exactly what I would say if this pastor said the wrong thing to me.

By the third and last month before the program my anxiety was gone but the unfortunate thing was I attended another service where I was told that this particular pastor had passed away a few days earlier. I was shocked! When the day came for me to go and preach I arrived at the church very early that morning. There was a black sheet covering the pastor's chair in the pulpit, which you can only imagine how I was feeling. I was met by one of the friendliest individuals, I have ever met, the associate pastor. He led me to the pastor study with all the other ministers, just so you know I was the only woman in there, after we prayed and he ran down the order of service they left me to have time alone. Before the associate left out I asked him which chair he wanted me to take in the pulpit, he said "oh you'll take the pastor seat, it's been thirty days and we are going to remove that covering for you". I couldn't believe it. He also made the comment that I would be the first to sit in the pastor's chair since he passed away. Now, I could take this in several directions but I won't. I do hope you get the picture? It is best for us to let God's will be done and to stay out of his way. Even when we think what we are doing is right, you just may need to stop and think. Nevertheless I preached, one woman received salvation and another stepped out and made her announcement as to the calling in her life! All l I could do in the midst of my praise was wonder as the old folk use to say, "Bet that pastor is turning over in his grave"!

Be not deceived God is not mocked for whatsoever a man soweth that he shall reap.

CHAPTER 11

A CHURCH JOURNEY

Being called into the ministry truly has been challenging. I remember when God called me, I was in my room on my knees praying and I heard the Lord as clear as a bell speak to me. I was afraid to tell anyone, I figured they would think, just as I was thinking, "this girl has bumped her head". So what I did was told the Lord if this is really you I'm hearing, please send confirmation from three people unknown to me and I will do your will.

It took almost two years before I received that third confirmation, but during those two years, I spent a lot time praying, I read the bible from Genesis to Revelations and I started rebuilding relationships that I destroyed. I was lead to call folks that I had offended and apologized. I knew they thought I was crazy and the funny thing was, I had forgotten most of the things that had happen but God brought them back to my remembrance. I thank him that he did because so many times we offend people and not realize that we have. We end up harboring those things on the inside. So, I know this was for them just as much as it was for me. Even though this was a rough time for me, I kept pressing on. The devil attacked me on every side. It wasn't until later that I knew without a doubt I was doing what God wanted me to do, because no devil in hell will bother you that bad unless God has a plan for your life.

I didn't say anything to my husband and then one day he came to me and asked me what was going on. He noticed a change in my life. When I explained to him what was going on, I remember us kneeling and praying at that moment together. We were asking God to protect and keep us in perfect peace through whatever we faced and he prayed that he would be supportive and understand every level of the ministry and would come in agreement with God according to what he had called me to do. Believe it or not, he has been one of my greatest supporters, and he has even kept me in line a few times. One thing he said to me and I'll never forget was "This is God's business and I feared him enough to know not to meddle in it".

It's funny how some folk think they know all about God's business, your business, and know nothing about their own business. Yet, I bet if you asked them a question about something in the bible they couldn't tell you. When I started out in the ministry, I sought after other licensed ministers and "seasoned ministers to teach me, but that was a joke. I learned more from folks "just passing by" as they called them than anyone else.

Once a neighbor and friend gave me a call to come and pray for an elderly woman in her neighborhood who was diagnosed with cancer. I want you to know I spent some of my best times with this woman and her family. I often wonder if that time was for me more than for them. The first time I went I prayed and ministered to her and her daughter. We had a wonderful time. Her daughter had the gift of prophecy which was very evident but she either didn't realize it or wasn't sure what it was. They asked me to come back a second time, but this time they had lunch prepared for me. It was at this time they shared with me a lot about their family and their religious background. They grew up not believing in Jesus. Eventually something changed in their lives and they did eventually accept him as their Savior. They also shared some very troubling experiences they had with some "church folk". The daughter was looking for a church home; she visited a church with one of her neighbors. She thought it was O.K. she didn't like all the singing and hollering they did, but she said it was tolerable. Than the neighbor asked the pastor to come and pray for her mother, that was O.K. too, but the bombshell came after the pastor finish praying, the neighbor insisted that they "pay" the minister for his time. She said they didn't mind giving him something but they were not the ones that asked him to come. I didn't say a one word. I was hurt because that was a mere reflection on all of us as ministers.

I didn't know if she was telling me this to let me know she was not paying me or she was waiting for my reaction. Then I immediately said, "Now you know you do not have to give me a thing", she said "oh I knew you didn't come for money the first time you came". Now, let me stop and tell you that this family was one of great means. It was very evident that they had money. They even shared pictures with me of the mother as a young model on a television show. I also knew the father (now deceased) held a high position with the government. So they were not people who were struggling in the finance department, but I'm so grateful that she could see and knew my intentions and that I was there only to spend time with them and comfort them.

The third time I was asked over, the mother was by this time bed ridden and very close to death. I sat on her bed and held her hand, we prayed and talked. She was ready to meet her maker and she couldn't wait to see her husband again which she believed in her heart he would be there to meet her also. Before I left her bedside she told her daughter to get the box off her dresser. In it was a very expensive bracelet and pearl earrings. She gave them to me and said she wanted me to have a part of her before she left. I cried! I couldn't believe it. I had never owned jewelry so expensive. Her daughter reached over grabbed my hand and said "I just heard a voice say to give you this also", she took a bracelet off her arms and gave it to me. She also made it very clear that if she had not heard that voice, I would not have that bracelet. It took her a long time to save the money for this particular bracelet and it was something she had wanted for years. What a Blessing! They did not owe me a dime to do what God had called me to do and which was to pray for the sick, feed the hungry and reach the lost! These were people who did not attend church but knew the love of God. What an impact they made on my life! In just this short time these women showed more love than any person I've ever met. No strings attached, just being friendly. I was a perfect stranger to them, and they were to me but what a relationship we built in just one month. We were of different nationality, different cultures but it did not matter!

CHAPTER 12

CHURCH ANYWHERE

Trusting God is an everyday practice. It is something that you do not have to wait and do on Sunday morning at church but you can trust him every minute, every second of the day. You can be in his presence every moment if you chose to. God is always near. Call on him! He will answer your prayers. He may not always answer in the way you want him to, but he will give you an answer. I'm so glad that I do not have to wait to get in the presence of people to feel his presence. What matters is what you are doing behind closed doors, when you are all alone. It's easy to praise God when the preacher or praise leader say's "Come on everybody, stand up and give God some praise", but behind closed doors after you just had a fight with your spouse, it gets hard to find peace like a river. Then on Sunday, you go and carry that entire burden, waiting just to leave it at the "alter" when you could have left it before you came. Sometimes you do not even have the chance to leave it because of the problems going on at the church.

Thank God I do not have to be confined to four walls to make me feel good or make me feel I've done my part and God is pleased. No, I can find peace in the mist of the storm wherever I am. I can help anybody wherever I am, pray for the sick anywhere, smile at someone passing by who is in return smiling at my husband when we're arguing. I can say "get thee behind me Satan" and he flees. I can help someone that is hurting and not judge them because they are not in church, just love them on purpose, that's what's pleasing to God. Sad to say but I couldn't find that in the church. When I was confined there, I spent more time in meetings, sleeping in service, and choir rehearsal. I often wondered whom was I helping doing that? I stayed more confused than anything. You didn't leave the church, you didn't talk about your church (even if they were wrong), you didn't visit other churches, all your money had to go to your church and only your church, what sense does that make? This is a type of bondage. If you do not believe me, go to your church Sunday and tell the preacher that you will not be there next Sunday, you'll going to visit the church down the street and see the reaction you get from your pastor, especially if you're a "high" tithing giver! It's like this for everybody, some denominations more than others.

Denomination, what in the world is that. To me it's like a secret organization that separates you from others. It's no different to me than Masons or Eastern Stars. And if you tell a Christian you are part of these organizations they'll eat you alive and really we're no different with our Baptist, Methodist, Church of God, Church of Christ, Pentecostal, Holiest, etc.

I have a friend who is a member of a Church who doesn't allow instruments in their church and to hear them tell it, if you have instruments in your church it's a sin. I have visited with her on several occasions and I'm always amused at how the preacher directs his sermons to the visitors as if you'll not a part of their church then you are a sinner. They want to baptize everyone that's not a member to make sure you are saved, and they'll do it that day, which I must say I do appreciate them being prepared for baptism if it's needed. Not like the Baptist who makes you wait several Sundays. But they shouldn't assume you are a sinner because you do not attend their church. I always laugh about it and my friend always tells me she wishes they wouldn't do that, but they do. What makes it funny is when we're leaving someone always wants to come to your house or invite you to their house for a quick bible study, I guess to pick your brain and see how much you know. I love it, I would love the challenge but for some reason they never come!

My friend's youngest sister was battling with cancer. She desired very much to be healed. I went and prayed for her many times. On one occasion she came to a service where I was the guest speaker. During the alter call, a very close friend of mine in the ministry laid hands on her and prayed for her healing. I'll never forget the words that the she spoke to her, she told her that God was going to heal her but to go and sin no more. She also told her that if she chose to go back into the world and continue doing what she had been doing that the sickness would revisit her, my friend's sister told me that day that she was going to start coming to church with me every Sunday and give God praise for what he had done. Unfortunately, she never came, she went back to her old ways and within the next year she passed away.

I wish then I would have preached and knew then what I know now. I knew in my heart that church was not her "thing". There were other ways she could have shown her gratitude towards God besides just going to church. She could have volunteered at the hospital, nursing home and even at the jail being a witness to how God can heal even cancer! I wished I had showed her that she could praise God just as well as at home. She didn't have transportation to get to church, and instead of me offering her a ride I fell down on being there for her. We could have gone witnessing on other days. The church her family attended was concerned only about her getting baptized more than anything, which she eventually was.

When she was put in hospice, I met her cousin. He was there to confess to her that even on her sick bed when it seems there's no hope, God can still heal but she had to believe. I knew when I heard him that there was something amazing about him. He shared with me that he had been healed from AIDs. I was so blessed just to talk with him and to hear how God had changed his life. He shared how his pastor came and prayed for him and spoke these words "you shall live and not die". We talked for a long while; it was one of those cherished moments where "life" was being spoken into my spirit.

At her funeral this same young man made remarks. He spoke about his healing and shared with the congregation of how he was very active in church playing the drums and writing plays etc. I remember his words being "I will beat those drums for the Lord as long as I live for his goodness to him". Right after his remarks the pastor or brother as they call themselves, got up and spoke negatively against his testimony all because he said that he played drums in the church. I was furious! I could have screamed. Not to mention I was already upset because the family asked the preacher, knowing that I was a minister, and I to sing sent word to me that I couldn't have music. I had to sing without music, which I already knew, and respected their beliefs regardless. He also said that I was to only sing, I couldn't say anything or try to preach and (as my friend put it) "you can't start speaking in tongues". So I was already fit to be tired! The church got quiet, no one said a word and after the service this cousin and his entire family left and did not stay to eat or fellowship with anyone. Oh, and let me tell you, I followed my instruction very well however, wouldn't you know one of her nurses got up to make remarks, preached, got the church stirred up and SPOKE IN TONGUES!!!! I was floored! All I could say was "Do It Jesus", and it's so funny that the only thing her two young sons talked about when they speak of their mother's funeral is this woman and what she said and did!

God is something else. They were so worried about what I would do, forgetting that God always have a ram in the bush. Now who do you think God was pleased with? This young man sharing his testimony giving God all the praise and glory or this preacher worried about some instrument in the church? Where was the Love? Would love make you hurt someone's feelings?!

CHAPTER 13

CHURCH CONFUSION

One Saturday, there was a knock at my door. When I opened the door there stood two women that were Jehovah's witnesses. I didn't know a whole lot about their faith but one thing I knew for sure was that if you were not a part of their group, one who attended Kingdom Hall, then you were a sinner and if they couldn't convert you they didn't want to have anything to do with you. I didn't have the time to invite them in but I did tell them that they could come back another time. Before they left they were very interested in knowing if I knew God? Yes! I told them. I also told them I knew his son Jesus. Oh Lord, what did I say that for? I opened a can of worms and didn't even know it. Those women lit into me like fire. They went on about Jesus being man just like us and so on and so on, but I thought that we had to accept Jesus to be saved and to see the Father. I knew that was the only way you could get to the Father was through his SON!

Well after we went back and forth, I told the women the conversation was over and we could agree to disagree and move on. To one of the women I said to her that she was my sister in Christ and that I loved her. She turned and looked at me and wanted to know what I meant by that. After talking a few more minutes, I explained myself, and she asked me for my telephone number so she could call me later. We spoke over several days, she told me of how she had been an atheist and when she moved here the first people she met were Jehovah's witnesses. After a while, her eyes became opened and we began to read and studied the bible together. She became interested very fast and she had so many questions about Jesus. She mainly wanted to stay in the Old Testament but I finally got her to reference the Old Testament to the New Testament, which made a world of difference to her. I'd like to believe that this woman found a new mind and that all that old stuff passed away and she became new.

Now I have to give the Jehovah witnessed their credit where credit is due. They are adamant about trying to convert people to their beliefs; however, what's sad about it is they are confusing those that are already confused. I blame us that know the word more than anything. We refuse to go knock on doors to talk to people about Jesus and when we do want to deliver a word we want to put on a program or conference, which ends up costing people money and not taking care of those who do not have ample transportation.

The belief of promoting a ministry is vital to the livelihood of that ministry. Local street rappers, for peat sake, even hustle for their money. So why aren't we out here hustling for God in the same manner. Problem is we are deafly afraid to do too much and/or do too little. We get in this mindset that believes that sister so in so isn't going to the party, so why do I? With this, we breathe life into the community that fosters and caters to the same ideas.

We need outreach ministries that will go out with the right messages not looking to gain anything but our giving. I remember once the Lord placed it on my heart to do a "Free Yard Sale". It took only one minute to explain to the members that we couldn't sale anything but we were to give it away. And it couldn't be junk stuff; it had to be nice things not torn or old. We sent out flyers all over, when the day came for the free sale, we hardly got any body there because they couldn't believe that all the items were free. Not only that we fed the people free hotdogs, chips, drinks and cookies. I remember one woman came from my home church and she got a dress that she to this day can't believe she didn't have to pay anything for it. After she went back and told everybody they wished they had come. They thought there was a catch to it. It's sad that we live in a society that can't expect a blessing without strings attached. Church should be about giving, assisting the community and going above and beyond to be there for others.

CHAPTER 14

CHURCH AT ITS BEST

In the experiences I have shared with you, it might sound as if I am being hard on the church or have given up on church. Not so! My problem is the people in these churches. I use to try and find that perfect church but I realize there is none. For me, I am looking for that place of worship that will not take all day to do God's will, his business, and the church that opens their doors to ALL people. One that will set up a fund raiser to help pay bills of those who are losing their homes or those that have lost their jobs, Those that will not taking struggling people monies to build bigger churches when there's no need. Think about it, there are churches that have asked members to pledge money to build larger dining halls in the church and then will turn around and make you pay a fee to use them after it was your money that help build it!

Let's look at the times we are living in. I would bet that there are families homeless that have given their money in the past to churches that won't even help them now. What about opening the doors to the church and letting them sleep in some of those dining halls instead of the streets? We are to bring our tithes in the storehouse, which I assume is enough to pay all church bills. This other debt is incurred unnecessarily.

Now the church want our tithes which is fine because it is a law and a principle we should abide by; however, they get to obtain more in the building fund offerings, a missionary offerings, which is suppose to help the sick, but do not allocate those funds respectively. You can sit in service and someone will testify that they have been sick and need medication that they can't afford and the church will take up their missionary offering and never make a move to help that person. You'll hear "Sweetie, we'll pray for you", Lord help us, that's why I do not mind having church in my home. All my bills are paid, I do not have to ask the members for anything to keep my lights or gas on. That is my responsibility to make sure that is always taken care of.

It is a blessing to be able to put all your money into an account that does nothing but help people. We pay pass due light bills, buy medicine, feed the elderly once a month and so on. It's fulfilling and I know that God is pleased with what we are doing. And guess what? I do not take a salary from the ministry, thank God for my job, I work! If I do not work, I do not eat! That reminds me of a pastor down the street from my home. He drove a Buick when he first got the church, after being there a while and receiving a very hefty salary, he brought a Mercedes. Was the Buick not good enough anymore? Why such an upgrade? Not long after that the church I was attending received a letter saying that his church was taking donations for his wife who was very ill and needed an operation. Now what's wrong with this picture!

Years ago I started sending money to one of the television ministries that have a lot of outreach programs in other countries. I've always wanted to help the missions over in Africa and other countries. I use to send money to four ministries until my husband said that was enough and made me choose only one to help. Well, not long ago my husband became ill. Due to all of the hospital and doctor bills we decided that we would refinance our home, take the equity revenue and pay off bills and my son's college tuition. With the banks experiencing major economic issues, we were turned down by several. Now to me that was a sign to leave it along. Not to go into debt. We had a comfortable mortgage payment and refinancing would have taken it well over what we wanted to pay. My husband jokingly made the comment, "all that money you sent to those ministries, maybe they will help us". I laughed, but that thought kept consuming me. I couldn't shake it off. I wasn't sure if this was going to be a blessing for us or a test for that ministry. So there I was, writing a letter to this ministry explaining all that we were going through and they politely wrote me back and said there was nothing they could do and sent me a C.D. entitled "Never Give Up". When I received that response I remember saying to myself, you do not have to worry, I will not!

It took me weeks before I shared that with my husband. We both laughed about it, but when I think about now, I wondered what they would have done if I had asked for all the money back that I had given them over the years. Of course it wouldn't have been near the amount I needed but it would have helped. Now ask me do I still support that ministry, yes I do without hesitation! I still believe in the work they're doing. I just pray they didn't fail a test!

Where are you church? Where is the one that walks the talk? Where is that faith-filled church that has the people of God at their point of interest? One that's not just dressed up beautiful and doesn't mind getting dirty while helping someone. Where are you church? Is there at least one that moves from within the four walls and not judge because someone is not of the same denomination? Is there a church that's embracing the poor, prison bound, the lost the sick, those that are outside of your four wall confinement! Where are you?

CONCLUSION

TRUE REVELATION

Let me tell you what I found out. I could spend more time going on and on with stories from my past, I could tell you more about the many times I was talked about at the church, how one member/deacon threatened me, to the point of physical harm. The numerous times pastors belittled me in front of the congregation, called out of my name by so-called Christian church folk, but I believe you get the gist of what I have disclosed. I do not have to be concerned about homosexual pastors, or those pastors that are full of filthy lucre, adulteress deacons, wild choir members, because they do not represent me, I know who I represent.

What I will tell you is that, all of this I at first blamed on the church but I through true revelation I realized, "It's not about the Church", or being "Confined to Four Walls", I am the church!

Me, you, all of us in our own spiritual bodies. It's not what folks have done to me or you; it's about what is being done in the response to those that are doing wrong. Everywhere I go, every step that I make I represent God's church. Not a choir, not the usher board, not the deacon board, motherboard or any other board. Just me! Out of all my experiences, whether I am in the street, in the beauty parlors, in someone's home, I am the church. Church is in my heart, my soul, my entire being. I represent the church, no matter where I go or what I'm doing in the church, church is in me. Thank God I can visit whatever denomination there is, because the building, the denomination means nothing, it's just what it is, a man made creation.

I pass along this thought, as long as I know who I am in Christ and stand firm on the solid foundation which is Jesus Christ, no one can turn my faith around. Church is in my living room everyday at the noonday hour. Church is in my car listening to my gospel music, church is when someone calls and needs prayer or encouragement. Church is wherever, whenever, and however God chooses to move. Church is when I remind my children of how good God is and has been to us. Church is every time we purchase items for our home or even for ourselves, we pray and give it back to God. I'm having church whenever I'm going through the fire and wrestling with the enemy. You see, I do not have to find the perfect church building because there is none. I am the church, I represent God! I am his daughter! Those of you that work in terrible and evil surroundings, you do not have to wait to get to that church building on Sunday and have the pastor deal with those demons you can deal with them yourselves right where you are. Do you think you have to wait until Sunday morning to tell God all about it? You do not. I can't tell you how many times I've heard "I can't wait to get to church Sunday, this week has been so hard", well who said you had to wait? Is God only moving on Sundays? You should not wait! I jokingly point out, the bible did say he rested on the Sabbath……, but with all jokes aside, his availability is in every minute of the day every day!

My business works with children and they tell us that we can't have any religious activities in our schedule. Well, that's why I'm glad I do not have religion, I have a relationship with God. When the children begin to act in a way that I cannot handle, I call on the Lord quickly. "Lord I need some help! I'll give that child a great big hug and whisper a prayer quickly!

So, when someone asks you what church do you belong to; tell them "I am the church"! If they ask you what denomination are you? Tell them, "I am a part of the family of God". If they ask you do you work in the church or hold a position, tell them "I work in the vineyard where the laborers are few", then ask them to join you and you both can be about God's business because…

It's more to it than just going to a Church, a four-wall confinement! It is about being the CHURCH that JESUS called.

It is time for the Church to awaken and BE!

------It is more than just Church!

www.ingramcontent.com/pod-product-compliance
Lightning Source LLC
LaVergne TN
LVHW091210080426
835509LV00006B/919